Australian Desert Animals

by Yara S. Mignon

Table of Contents

Chapter I

Deserts Down Under

Australia is the driest continent in the world. It has 10 deserts.

All deserts are very dry. They are hot during the day, and cold at night. But many plants and animals have **adapted** to life in the desert.

People live in the Australian desert, too. The Aboriginal *(a-buh-RIJ-i-nuhl)* people have lived in the Australian desert for 40,000 years.

Some people work as desert rangers. A ranger's job is to care for the land and the animals that live there. ⊙

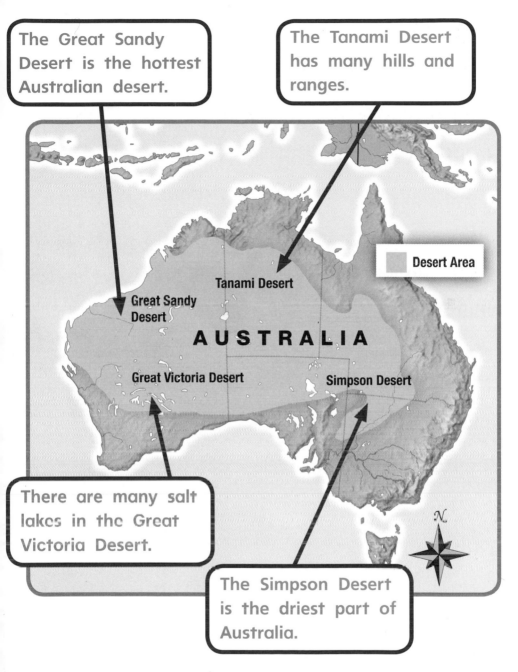

The Great Sandy Desert is the hottest Australian desert.

The Tanami Desert has many hills and ranges.

Desert Area

Tanami Desert

Great Sandy Desert

AUSTRALIA

Great Victoria Desert

Simpson Desert

There are many salt lakes in the Great Victoria Desert.

The Simpson Desert is the driest part of Australia.

⌖ Australia's four largest deserts cover most of the country.

Chapter 2
Amazing Desert Animals

The red kangaroo lives in the Australian desert. A female can carry its young in a pouch, or pocket, on its stomach.

Kangaroos are **marsupials**. There are more than 200 kinds of marsupials that live in or near Australia.

Only male red kangaroos are red. Females have gray on their backs. ⊕

⊙ The numbat often hides in hollow logs.

Most desert marsupials, such as the numbat, are small. They can dig into the sand and hide under rocks or in trees.

Most marsupials are active at night. In the day, they hide from the hot sun.

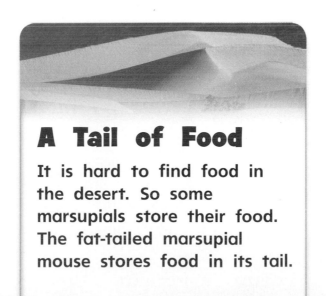

A Tail of Food

It is hard to find food in the desert. So some marsupials store their food. The fat-tailed marsupial mouse stores food in its tail.

Some animals that live in the Australian desert come from distant places. Explorers brought camels to the desert more than 150 years ago.

Camels don't need much water. That has helped them adapt to life in the Australian desert.

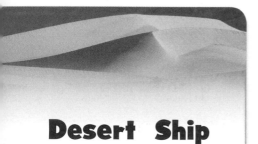

Desert Ship

People used to ride camels across the Australian desert. Camels were called "ships of the desert." Now cars and railroads have become more common.

◑ In some areas, there are 100 camels for every one red kangaroo.

A dingo is a wild dog. ⌒

Aboriginal people brought dingoes from Asia around 10,000 years ago. Some dingoes were kept as pets.

Pets that escape are called feral animals. Feral animals are a big problem because they eat small marsupials. Now there are fewer small marsupials, such as the bilby.

Bilbies were once found all over Australia. Now only small groups live in a few areas. ⊃

Chapter 3
Desert Birds

Desert birds are amazing desert animals. The emu is a big bird that can run at 30 miles (50 kilometers) per hour! That is faster than any person can run. An emu has wings, but it does not fly.

Like emus, many Australian desert birds move around from place to place. These birds come to the desert when it rains because the lakes fill up. When the lakes are dry, the birds move away.

Emus can grow as tall as an adult person. ⊃

Some birds hunt many other animals. The wedge-tailed eagle is the biggest hunting bird in Australia. Each eagle hunts in its own area. It will usually not go far beyond its area.

The wedge-tailed eagle has wings that are more than 2 yards (2 meters) wide. ⮌

Chapter 4
Desert Reptiles and Amphibians

Most Australian snakes are **venomous**. This means their bite can hurt or kill other animals. The taipan is Australia's toughest and most venomous desert snake.

⏾ A taipan can grow to 11 feet (3.3 meters). That is longer than a car!

A lizard called the thorny devil changes color to match the sand. It looks dangerous. But it only eats ants.

The thorny devil can eat 3,000 ants in one meal!

The water-holding frog goes for lengthy periods without leaving its burrow. It only comes out when it rains. Sometimes it doesn't rain for many years.

The water-holding frog looks like a balloon because it holds water under its skin. ➲

Chapter 5
Desert Arachnids

Spiders are **arachnids**. There are hundreds of kinds of spiders in the Australian desert.

Most spiders live on webs they make. But there are not many places to build a web in the desert. Some desert spiders, such as mouse spiders, live in burrows.

The female mouse spider never leaves her burrow. The male leaves only when it rains.

↻ A mouse spider is about as big as a baby mouse.

Scorpions are also arachnids. They hunt at night for spiders and other insects to eat. Some scorpions also eat snakes, mice, and lizards.

Hide and Seek

Some arachnids have body colors that blend into the land around them. This hides and protects them.

This scorpion has its stinger raised in warning. It is ready to sting. ↻

Many animals have adapted to life in the Australian deserts. They have learned to store food and drink less water. They burrow to stay cool. They blend in with the desert to stay safe. These animals have made the Australian desert their home.

⬇ The woma python lives in Australia's Tanami Desert.

Glossary

adapted *(uh-DAPT-ed)* changed
(page 2)

arachnids *(uh-RACK-nids)* arthropods (not insects) with four pairs of legs and a body in two parts *(page 12)*

marsupials *(mar-SOO-pee-uhlz)* animals that carry their young in a pouch *(page 4)*

venomous *(VEN-uh-muhs)* poisonous *(page 10)*

Index

Comprehension Check

Retell

Use an Author's Purpose Chart and the photos to help you retell the information in this book.

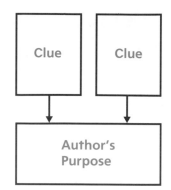

Think and Compare

1. Turn to page 7. Why are feral animals a problem in Australia? *(Summarize)*

2. What animals would you like to see in an Australian desert? Explain. *(Analyze)*

3. Which deserts do you know about that are not in Australia? How are they alike or different from the desert in Australia? *(Evaluate)*